ALGEBRA
FOR THE
URBAN STUDENT

ALGEBRA
FOR THE
URBAN STUDENT

Using Stories to Make Algebra Fun and Easy

CANAA LEE

iUniverse, Inc.
Bloomington

ALGEBRA FOR THE URBAN STUDENT
Using Stories to Make Algebra Fun and Easy

iUniverse books may be ordered through booksellers or by contacting:

iUniverse
1663 Liberty Drive
Bloomington, IN 47403
www.iuniverse.com
1-800-Authors (1-800-288-4677)

ISBN: 978-1-4759-1555-6 (sc)
ISBN: 978-1-4759-1556-3 (ebk)

Printed in the United States of America

iUniverse rev. date: 05/07/2012

CONTENTS

PREFACE

In 2004, I was a high school math teacher at Little Rock Central High School. As a part of the campus improvement plan, Central High School wanted to promote literacy across the curriculum. Every content area teacher needed to utilize reading strategies. The question most math teachers ask themselves is "how do I teach reading in my math class . . . why do I have to teach reading in math?"

It was challenging enough teaching the concepts and now we were expected to teach reading too! Often times I found myself reading and explaining everything in the book. This took a lot of time and was also very exhausting. Unfortunately, this did not help students comprehend the material. In addition, encouraging students to do homework was almost impossible. Usually, from the time students left class until they got ready to do their homework, they had forgotten almost everything we talked about in class. What is a teacher to do?

The most effective way for me to incorporate reading in algebra was to select the topics that had a common theme and infuse them into story. The vocabulary in the textbook was advanced for my students; as a result, they found the concepts difficult and were easily frustrated. For example, there is a unit called "Family of Equations and Inequalities." Now, my students would learn the main algebra topics and learn the math skills at the same time!

As an expert algebra teacher, I understand that algebra is based on the concept of a line. However, there are many skills students must master in order to master the concept. Through the use of culturally relevant stories and utilizing the graphing calculator daily, my students were finally able to make the connection between skills and the concepts. The stories help students follow along throughout the whole unit. There are questions asked along the way so students are able to "demonstrate your understanding". The assessments are directly related to the unit so students have the opportunity to incorporate the graphing calculator in almost every unit.

Writing units and creating real world performance assessments required a lot of hours outside of the normal work day. However, when I put my creative hat on, there was no stopping me. It was imperative for me to show my students that algebra is more than just a "bunch of letters and numbers with no meaning." For example, relating parabolas to a hill or a valley is an idea every student can relate; illustrating the relationship between linear equations and inequalities helps students understand that everything in algebra is related and is not really that hard at all!

My algebra students inspired *Algebra for the Urban Student*. It started off as just a collection of units for my students so I could ensure that were exposed to and mastered all the topics for the assessments. Parents commented on homework assignments because they could now help their children with their homework because it was easy to understand and follow without even stepping foot in my class! My students liked coming to class because they wanted to know the next story I had written. For the first time, many students understood their homework and could complete their assignments. Also, students were improving their reading and comprehension skills in both English and algebra! I had written enough units and assessments to write a book. Textbooks are designed for math teachers and professors; *Algebra for the Urban Student* is intended for the common student.

FOREWORD

Algebra and Urban Students: The Gateway to Success in the 21st Century

A critical and strategic examination of the social science and popular literature concerning urban students highlights a distressing depiction of their mathematics achievement. This trend disheartens me even more because of the disproportionate number of Black and Latino kids in urban schools who are not being adequately prepared in mathematics. According to the National Assessment of Education, a division of the U.S. Department of Education, over 60 percent of this population has not reached basic proficiency levels in their mathematics subjects at the middle and high school levels, particularly in Algebra. This occurs at a time when our nation has made an increased emphasis on STEM (Science, Technology, Engineering and Mathematics) in secondary and postsecondary education to main our position as a world superpower. Increasing the number of urban students who are successful in Algebra and other high-level mathematics courses has to become an educational imperative. This educational investment into our urban students is very likely to yield great returns.

Algebra and the Urban Student: Using Stories to Make Algebra Easy and Fun makes an important and much needed contribution to a highly important educational issue in urban schools and beyond. Canaa Lee has assembled a powerful collection of chapters that make Algebra relevant and achievable for urban students. Additionally, the activities will allow urban students to understand that Algebra can be fun. I am particularly excited about this book because it allows hands-on activities for educational practitioners to build the mathematics skill set of our students. It is my hope that this book will encourage others to produce books and other written contributions that are hands-on and able to be easily implemented into Algebra classrooms. Further, I hope that educators will truly see the value of this book for its potential in raising the achievement levels of urban students in Algebra.

In closing, I commend Canaa Lee for putting this book together. These chapters bring thought-provoking and real-world perspectives to Algebra. As a result, I will certainly add this book to my library. I hope you enjoy!

Chance W. Lewis, Ph.D.
Carol Grotnes Belk Distinguished Professor of Urban Education
College of Education
The University of North Carolina at Charlotte
E-mail: chance.lewis@uncc.edu
Web: http://www.chancewlewis.com

INTRODUCTION

This book is inspired by the students I teach. So many times students do so well in class, but when they leave my classroom they have forgotten everything or are confused as to how to do their homework. My students would say to me, "I wish I could stick you in pocket and take you home with me." Because I heard this so frequently from them, I started writing stories for my students. The activities are guided practice exercises so they would have a "navigation system" to guide them through the entire assignment. It is closest thing to having me right there with them as they were doing their homework. My stories became a hit with the students and parents alike. I have written enough stories to compile them all into a book. My book, *Algebra for the Urban Student,* takes into consideration the challenges students in the math classroom and use cultural relevance to help them wrap their minds around abstract concepts so they are able to experience success and confidence in their math class!

CHAPTER 1

FAMILY OF EQUATIONS AND INEQUALITIES

This unit is designed for students to learn how to solve linear equations, linear inequalities, absolute value equations and inequalities all the same time. There's no need to teach them independently, rather teach them collectively to show students how they are all related.

To show the relationship between equations and inequalities, we have taken the equations from Activity One and turned them into inequalities in Activity Two. The technique is the same with one major difference: The Number Line!

ACTIVITY ONE

Solve the following equations for x.

1. $x + 3 = 6$

2. $x + 5 = 3$

3. $x - 4 = 7$

4. $x - 6 = -8$

5. $x + 3 = -6$

6. $x + 7 = 3$

7. $6 - 2x = -4$

8. $4x + 8 = -8$

9. $8x + 1 = 25$

10. $7x - 30 = 19$

11. $6x + 1 = -2$

12. $-7 - 4x = 13$

13. $3x - 1 = 1$

ACTIVITY TWO

Solve each of the following inequalities. Graph each of them on the number line.

1. $x + 3 < 6$

2. $x + 5 \leq 3$

3. $x - 4 \leq 7$

4. $x - 6 < -8$

5. $x + 3 \geq -6$

6. $x + 7 > 3$

7. $6 - 2x < -4$

8. $4x + 8 \geq -8$

9. $8x + 1 \leq 25$

10. $7x - 30 < 19$

11. $6x + 1 \leq -2$

12. $-7 - 4x < 13$

13. $3x - 1 > 1$

HOMEWORK

Graph each of the following inequalities on a number line.

1. x < 2

2. x ≥ 3

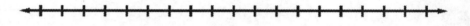

3. 4 < x

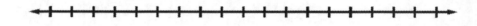

4. -1 ≥ x

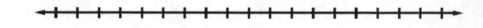

5. x < 0

Solve each of the following inequalities. Graph each of them on the number line.

6. x + 2 < 5

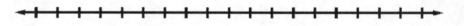

7. x − 3 ≤ 1

8. x + 7 ≥ 1

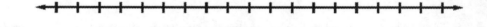

9. 3x − 6 > 3

10. 2x + 1 > 5

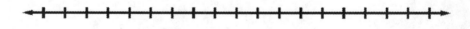

11. 2x − 3 ≤ 7

12. 3x + 2 ≤ 8

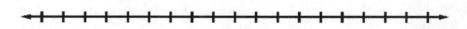

13. 5 − 4x < 11

OBJECTIVE

Students will be able to solve absolute value equations and absolute value inequalities.

Students will be able to:

- Define absolute value
- Solve absolute value equations using a number line
- Write a sentence to describe the absolute value equations
- Solve absolute value inequalities
- Solve absolute value inequalities using a number line
- Write a sentence to describe the absolute value inequalities

ABSOLUTE VALUE EQUATIONS

$|x| = 3$ is the same thing as $|x - 0| = 3$. $|x - 0| = 3$ means the distance between x and 0 is 3 units.

1. What numbers are 3 units from zero?

   So $x = 3$ and $x = -3$ are solutions to $|x| = 3$. There are two solutions, $x = 3$ and $x = -3$.

   $|x| = -5$ is NOT possible. We do not talk about negative distance.
   $|x| = -5$ has NO SOLUTION.

   $|x + 2| = 7$ is the same thing as $|x - (-2)| = 7$. $|x - (-2)| = 7$ means the distance between x and -2 is 7 units.

2. What numbers are 7 units from zero?

   $|x - 3| = 4$ is the same thing as $|x - (+3)| = 4$. $|x - (+3)| = 4$ means the distance between x and 3 is 4 units.

3. What numbers are 4 units from 3?

   $|6 - x| = 7$ is the same thing as $|-x - (-6)| = 7$.
   $|-x - (-6)| = 7$ means the distance between -x and -6 is 7 units.

4. What numbers are 7 units from -6?

   Reminder: *Don't forget to divide both solutions by -1 because x is negative.*

   $|2x - (+1)| = 3$ is the distance between 2x and 1 is 3 units.

5

ABSOLUTE VALUE INEQUALITIES

Here's an example: $|x| < 3$

Let's look at it on the number line: (open circles on 3 and -3)

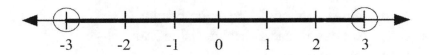

1. What two inequalities are represented?

    Let's look at another example: $|x| \geq 3$

    Let's look at it on the number line: (closed circles on 3 and -3)

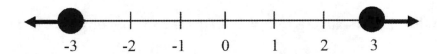

ACTIVITY THREE

Absolute Value Equations. Write a sentence that describes the absolute value equation. Illustrate the equation on the number line. Solve the absolute value equation.

1. $|x| = 4$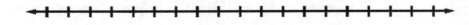

2. $|x| = -8$

3. $|x| = 7$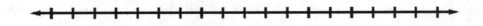

4. $|x - 2| = 3$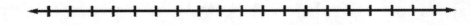

5. $|x + 3| = 4$

6. $|x - 4| = 1$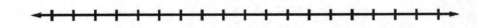

7. $|x + 1| = 2$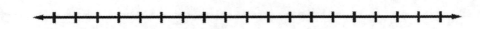

8. $|2 - x| = 5$

9. $|6 - x| = 7$

10. $|x - 7| = 5$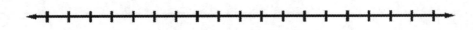

11. $|2x - 1| = 3$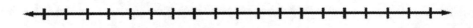

12. $|5x - 7| = 3$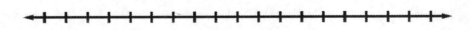

13. $|3x - 2| = 6$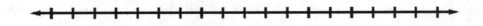

ACTIVITY FOUR

Absolute Value Inequalities. Write a sentence that describes the absolute value inequality. Illustrate the inequality on the number line. Solve the absolute value inequality.

1. $|x| < 4$

2. $|x| > -8$

3. $|x| \geq 7$

4. $|x - 2| \leq 3$

5. $|x + 3| < 4$

6. $|x - 4| < 1$

7. $|x + 1| > 2$

8. $|2 - x| \leq 5$

9. $|6 - x| \leq 7$

10. $|x - 7| \geq 5$

11. $|2x - 1| \geq 3$

12. $|5x - 7| < 3$

13. $|3x - 2| > 6$

REVIEW FOR TEST

Graph each of the following inequalities.

1. 3x – y < 8

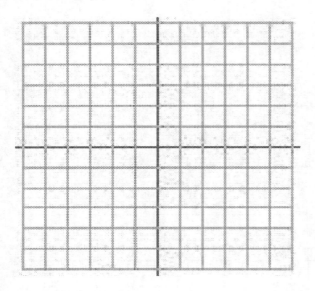

3. y ≥ 1/3x – 5

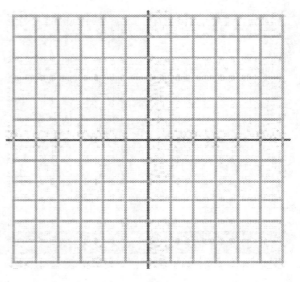

2. y ≥ 4x – 2

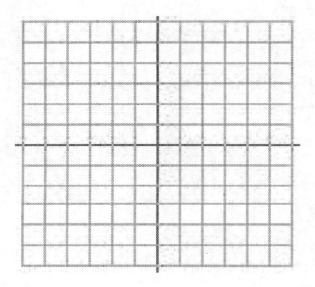

4. y – 4x ≤ -3

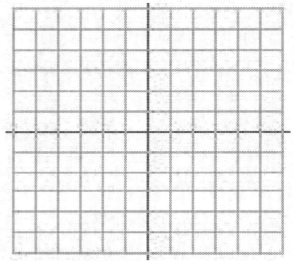

Graph each of the following inequalities on a number line.

5. $x + 3 < 6$

6. $6x + 1 \leq -2$

7. $x < 0$

8. $6 - 2x \leq -8$

9. $3x - 2 \geq 7x - 10$

ABSOLUTE VALUE EQUATIONS

1. Describe the absolute equation in a sentence

2. Solve the absolute value equation using a number line.

3. Write the compound inequality that represents the absolute value equation.

10. $|x| = 5$

11. $|x - 7| = 5$

12. $|6 - x| = 7$

13. $|2x - 3| = 9$

14. $|5x - 2| = 11$

COMBINED INEQUALITIES

15. $1 < x + 3 \leq 5$

16. $3 + 2x \geq 15$ or $4x - 2 < 0$

17. $-7 \leq 3 - 2x < 13$

ABSOLUTE VALUE INEQUALITIES

18. $|x| \geq 3$

19. $|x| < 5$

20. $|x + 2| < 5$

21. $|x - 3| \leq 1$

22. $|2x + 1| > 5$

23. $|5 - 4x| < 11$

CHAPTER 2

GRAPH THAT INEQUALITY!

2x – 6y > 12: Answer the following questions about the given inequality.

1. Determine whether the graph is of a solid line or a dashed line. How do you know?

2. Solve the inequality for y.

3. Make a table and choose three points from the table in the calculator to write in your table.

4. Graph the three points on the graph that is provided and draw a line through them.

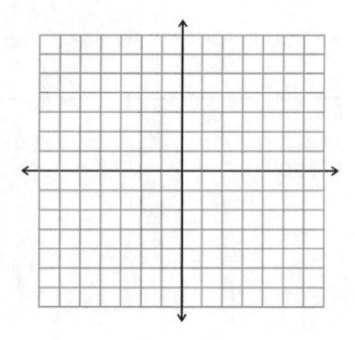

5. How do you determine where to shade the graph (use the test point (0,0))?

6. What happens when you choose a point in the shaded region?

7. What happens when you choose a point in the un-shaded region?

8. What happens when you choose a point on the line?

CHAPTER 3

HELP ME! I NEED TO FIND MY EQUATION!

Hey! My name is Slope. My friends call me "M." My friend is Ordered Pair. We are having a bad day because we can not find our equation. Do you think you can help us find our equation? Ordered Pair and M are going to tell you how to find their equation. Please follow along carefully because they really need your help.

Ok, we are going to let **m = 3** and let the ordered pair be (0,-4). They fit into the slope-intercept formula: $y = mx + b$. Well, we know that M is a nickname for Slope. Ordered Pair has two friends, X and Y. The first number is X and the second number is Y. So x = 0 and y = -4. Slope, x, and y have a place the slope-intercept formula.

Let's look at the formula: $y = mx + b$. Replace the y with the -4, replace the m with the 3, and replace the x with the 0. So now we have $-4 = 3(0) + b$. Solve this equation for b. What does b equal? _____

Now, we know that m = 3 and b = -4. When we write the equation, we get $y = 3x - 4$. M and Ordered Pair are happy! They found their equation! So, do you think you can do it on your own?

Here's one for you: m = -2 and the ordered pair is (-3, 5). Help us find our equation!

Ok, a few more won't hurt:

1) M = 0.5; (0, 9)

2) M = -2; (-8, -6)

3) M = -0.5; (3, -7)

Help us find our equations!

Thank you very much for helping us in our desperate attempts to find our equations. But there is another problem we need help with. Ordered Pair has another ordered pair as a friend. We need your help to find Slope and the equation! Can you help us? We will do our best to give you clues. Are you ready? OK, let's go . . .

Here are the two ordered pairs, (0, 7) and (1,-5). We need help finding Slope first. Well, we know that Slope is a little explanation. He is the change in y divided by the change in x. So, we need to subtract the y-values and divide them by the difference in the x-values. Does that sound like a plan? So, let's see what we get . . .

The 2 y-values are 7 and -5. Let's subtract them: 7 – (-5) = 12. Ok, now let's subtract the x-values: 0 – 1 = -1. Slope is 12/-1; m = -12. Yeah, we found Slope!

We have 2 ordered pairs. Which one do we use to find the equation? Let's try (0, 7) first: m = -12 and the ordered pair is (0, 7). Well, x is 0, m is -12, and y is 7. They all have a place in the slope-intercept formula, $y = mx + b$.

Now we can write $7 = -12(0) + b$. What is b? _____. My equation is _____.

What about the other ordered pair? Let's use her and see what happens . . .

This time, y is -5, x is 1 and m is -12. They all have a place in $y = mx + b$.

Now we can write $-5 = -12(1) + b$. What is b? _____. My equation is _____.

What do you notice about the two equations?

So, here's a few for you to do:

1) (9, 0) and (-6, 2). Remember to find my friend, Slope first.

2) (2, -4) and (-3, -5)

3) (4, 3) and (0, 0)

CHECK YOUR UNDERSTANDING

M and Ordered Pair want to find their equation. We are going to let m = -1 and Ordered Pair is (9, -7). M and B fit into the equation y = mx + b. We have M so we need B.

    a.   What is y? _____. b. What is x? _____. c. What is m? _____.

    d.   Substitute y, x, and m into the equation: _____ = _____ * _____ + b.

    e.   Now you need to solve the equation for b. What does b equal? _____

    f.   What is my equation? y = _____ * x + _____.

1.   M = -0.25; (-3, 5)

    a.   What is y? _____. b. What is x? _____. c. What is m? _____.

    d.   Substitute y, x, and m into the equation: _____ = _____ * _____ + b.

    e.   Now you need to solve the equation for b. What does b equal? _____

    f.   What is my equation? y = _____ * x + _____.

2.   M = 4; (2, -6)

    a.   What is y? _____. b. What is x? _____. c. What is m? _____.

    d.   Substitute y, x, and m into the equation: _____ = _____ * _____ + b.

    e.   Now you need to solve the equation for b. What does b equal? _____

    f.   What is my equation? y = _____ * x + _____.

3.   M = -1; (-8, -5)

    a.   What is y? _____. b. What is x? _____. c. What is m? _____.

    d.   Substitute y, x, and m into the equation: _____ = _____ * _____ + b.

    e.   Now you need to solve the equation for b. What does b equal? _____

    f.   What is my equation? y = _____ * x + _____.

4. M = 1/3; (-4, 0)

    a. What is y? _____. b. What is x? _____. c. What is m? _____.

    d. Substitute y, x, and m into the equation: _____ = _____ * _____ + b.

    e. Now you need to solve the equation for b. What does b equal? _____

    f. What is my equation? y = _____ * x + _____.

Now, we need to find the equation when there are two ordered pairs. So let's say we have (0, 6) and (2,3).

    1) What are the two y-values? _____

    2) Subtract the two y-values. Tell me what you get: _____

    3) What are the two x-values? _____

    4) Subtract the two x-values. Tell me what you get: _____

    5) Take the answer from #2 and divide it by the answer in #4: _____. This answer is the slope.

    Find the equation: y = _____ * x + _____.

Problem 1: (-3,-6) and (1, 3)

    1) What are the two y-values? _____

    2) Subtract the two y-values. Tell me what you get: _____

    3) What are the two x-values? _____

    4) Subtract the two x-values. Tell me what you get: _____

    5) Take the answer from #2 and divide it by the answer in #4: _____. This answer is the slope.

    Find the equation: y = _____ * x + _____.

Problem 2: (0, 0) and (-4,-8)

    1) What are the two y-values? _____

2) Subtract the two y-values. Tell me what you get: _____

3) What are the two x-values? _____

4) Subtract the two x-values. Tell me what you get: _____

5) Take the answer from #2 and divide it by the answer in #4: _____. This answer is the slope.

Find the equation: y = _____ * x + _____.

Problem 3: (-3,-9) and (-2,-5)

1) What are the two y-values? _____

2) Subtract the two y-values. Tell me what you get: _____

3) What are the two x-values? _____

4) Subtract the two x-values. Tell me what you get: _____

5) Take the answer from #2 and divide it by the answer in #4: _____. This answer is the slope.

Find the equation: y = _____ * x + _____.

Problem 4: (3, 3) and (5, 0)

1) What are the two y-values? _____

2) Subtract the two y-values. Tell me what you get: _____

3) What are the two x-values? _____

4) Subtract the two x-values. Tell me what you get: _____

5) Take the answer from #2 and divide it by the answer in #4: _____. This answer is the slope.

Find the equation: y = _____ * x + _____.

CHAPTER 4

DO YOU REALLY KNOW YOUR SLOPE?

Here is a list of vocabulary words you need to be familiar with for this assignment. For each of the following terms, define each of them in your own words:

1. Describe

2. Slope

3. Slope-intercept form

4. $Y = mx + b$

5. Identify

6. y-intercept

7. ordered pair

8. graph

9. equation

10. determine

11. increasing

12. decreasing

13. list

14. steepness

Solve each of the following equations for y.

1. $x + y = 4$
2. $-3x + y = -8$
3. $4x - y = 2$

4. $x + 3y = -12$
5. $-2x - 3y = -12$
6. $5x + 10y = 27$
7. $2x + 3y = -15$
8. $-5x - 2y = -20$
9. $7y = x + 2$
10. $-x = -9y + 3$
11. $3y + 18x = -6$
12. $-9x = y + 9$
13. $27y = 3x - 21$

For each of the equations listed above, you are to answer each of the following statements for each of the 13 problems.

1. Describe how to solve each equation (in words)
2. Solve each equation for y.
3. Write each equation in slope-intercept form ($y = mx + b$)
4. Identify the slope in each equation.
5. Identify the y-intercept in each equation. Write the y-intercept as an ordered pair.
6. Graph each equations using the slope and the y-intercept
7. Determine whether the slope increases or decreases.
8. List the equations in order by steepness. In other words, list the equation with the steepest slope first down to the equation that has the least steep slope.

GRADING

- This assignment is worth 100 points
- Each graph is to be graphed on graph paper. Each graph is to be with each problem. This means you will have to cut the graph paper and glue it or staple it onto your paper. There is a 20 point deduction for not using graph paper.
- For each problem, you must answer every question
- Every question must be written, numbered and the answer is written below the statement. There is a 20 point deduction for not writing the statements and numbering each of them.
- Every answer must be clear and concise (no short cuts)
- Solutions should be modeled after the given example
- The correct answer heading must be on your assignment. No heading, no grade.
- Question 8 should be answered last. Answer questions 1-7 for each equation first, then go back and list the equations in order from steepest to least steep.

CHAPTER 5

USING ALGEBRA IN EVERYDAY LIFE

I bet you never thought how you use algebra outside of your algebra class. Say you are buying gas at the pump. Gas is really high right now. Let's say that it's $3.79 per gallon. That's math! How about the weather? How about the business section with all those numbers? Well, in this project, we are going to use some the algebra concepts we talked about in class and apply them to our everyday living.

This project is worth 200 points. It is due on _____. Late projects will not be accepted under any circumstances. You can turn the project in early, but not late. NO EXCEPTIONS. We will work on the project in class.

For this project, you will need the following materials:

- Newspaper
- Construction paper
- Scissors
- Glue/glue sticks
- Calculator
- Rulers
- Markers/colored pencils
- Pens/pencil
- Textbook (optional)*

Here are some of the mathematical concepts that you are to utilize:

- Relations and functions (i.e. weather, sports stats, business . . .)
- Function rule (i.e. sales paper, car ads, advertisements . . .)
- Statistics (bar graphs, scatter plots, circle graphs . . .)
- Real number system
- Inequalities
- Ratios and proportions
- Rate of change
- Compound inequalities

You are to have 10 entries. You will cut out an ad from the newspaper and glue it on construction. You are allowed to have more than one ad on a sheet of construction. All work must be neat. You will have to decide which algebra concept that you are going to apply to the advertisement. You will receive a daily grade for working in class. That is 100 points a week.

Each entry must include the following:

- You must use 10 different ads from different parts of the paper (i.e. business, sale ads, weather, sports, advertisements . . .)
- You must use mathematical concepts relating to algebra
- Use correct mathematics
- Create an example or a description

GRADING RUBRIC

Your grade for this project will be judged on the following criteria:

Ad #1:

Entry is neat, organized and creative.................................... (5 points) _____
Used the appropriate algebra topic.................................... (5 points) _____
Used the correct computation.. (5 points) _____
Gave description or example .... (5 points) _____

Ad #2:

Entry is neat, organized and creative.................................... (5 points) _____
Used the appropriate algebra topic.................................... (5 points) _____
Used the correct computation.. (5 points) _____
Gave description or example .... (5 points) _____

Ad #3:

Entry is neat, organized and creative.................................... (5 points) _____
Used the appropriate algebra topic.................................... (5 points) _____
Used the correct computation.. (5 points) _____
Gave description or example .... (5 points) _____

Ad #4:

Entry is neat, organized and creative.................................... (5 points) _____
Used the appropriate algebra topic.................................... (5 points) _____
Used the correct computation.. (5 points) _____
Gave description or example .... (5 points) _____

Ad #5:

Entry is neat, organized and creative.................................... (5 points) _____
Used the appropriate algebra topic.................................... (5 points) _____
Used the correct computation.. (5 points) _____
Gave description or example .... (5 points) _____

Ad #6:

Entry is neat, organized and creative.................................... (5 points) _____
Used the appropriate algebra topic.................................... (5 points) _____

Used the correct computation. . . . . (5 points) _____

Gave description or example . . . . (5 points) _____

Ad #7:

Entry is neat, organized and creative. . . . . (5 points) _____

Used the appropriate algebra topic. . . . . (5 points) _____

Used the correct computation. . . . . (5 points) _____

Gave description or example . . . . (5 points) _____

Ad #8:

Entry is neat, organized and creative. . . . . (5 points) _____

Used the appropriate algebra topic. . . . . (5 points) _____

Used the correct computation. . . . . (5 points) _____

Gave description or example . . . . (5 points) _____

Ad #9:

Entry is neat, organized and creative. . . . . (5 points) _____

Used the appropriate algebra topic. . . . . (5 points) _____

Used the correct computation. . . . . (5 points) _____

Gave description or example . . . . (5 points) _____

Ad #10:

Entry is neat, organized and creative. . . . . (5 points) _____

Used the appropriate algebra topic. . . . . (5 points) _____

Used the correct computation. . . . . (5 points) _____

Gave description or example . . . . (5 points) _____

Total: . . . . (200 points) _____

CHAPTER 6

PROJECT FOR GEOMETRY

This project is due on _____. **Late projects will not be accepted under any circumstances. You can turn the project in early, but not late. NO EXCEPTIONS.** We will work on the project in class. This is a 3-part project. Part I requires you to write a 2-page paper on a topic in the history of mathematics relating to algebra (if possible). No two people are allowed to have the same topic.

You must use 12-point font, double-spaced with one inch margins.

All topics must be **approved by me** before you can work on it. First come, first serve. (*All approvals are due by* _____)

- Discuss major contributions to the mathematical world
- Describe what you have learned
- Describe the significance of algebra
- Students will sign up for a day to give a 2-3 minute presentation (i.e. power point, speech, poem, poster . . .)

**** The paper is worth 100 points ****

PART II   GEOMETRY IN REAL LIFE, "LIVING IN A 3-D WORLD"

You will be surprised how much "math" is just sitting around your house. Most of you carry some things to school everyday: cell phone, body spray, CDs, I-pod, candy, sodas, etc . . . Well, we are going to put all these items to good "geometric" use.

Students need to collect five 2-D and 3-D objects around the house. Each student gathers 5 objects. Here is a list of possible objects you can use. *You are welcome to use items that are not on the list:*

- CDs
- CD case
- Basketball
- Baseball
- Milk Carton
- Shoe Box
- Picture frame
- Cologne/perfume box
- Soda can
- Soup can
- Orange juice carton
- Cereal box
- Cereal bowl
- I-pod
- Tissue box
- Shoe box
- Book

You will need the following materials for this part of the project:

- Disposal camera or digital camera
- Scissors
- Construction paper
- Glue stick
- Ruler
- Tape measure
- Markers/colored pencils
- Pens/pencils
- Formula chart
- Textbook*

Students will be required to:

- Take pictures of each of the items that you have selected to use.
- Determine whether the objects are 2-D or 3-D.

It is your task to **find the perimeter and area** of the 2-D figures and find the **surface area and volume** of the 3-D figures.

In addition, you are to write a description or create a situation to represent your figure.

You are to have five entries. Each entry must include the following:

- Photograph on construction paper
- Formula(s)
- Calculations with appropriate units
- Description or situation
- Neat, accurate and creative

**** Part II of the project is worth 100 points ****

PART III "USING ALGEBRA IN EVERYDAY LIFE"

I bet you never thought how you use algebra outside of your algebra class. Say you are buying gas at the pump. Gas is really high right now. Let's say that it $3.79 per gallon. That's math! How about the weather? How about the business section with all those numbers? Well, in this project, we are going to use some the algebra concepts we talked about in class and apply them to our everyday living.

For this part of the project, you will need the following materials:

- Newspaper
- Construction paper
- Scissors
- Glue/glue sticks
- Calculator

- Rulers
- Markers/colored pencils
- Pens/pencil
- Textbook (optional)*

Here are some of the mathematical concepts that you are to utilize:

- Relations and functions
- Function rule
- Statistics
- Real number system
- Inequalities
- Ratios and proportions
- Rate of change
- Compound inequalities

You are to have 5 entries. You will cut out an ad from the newspaper and glue it on construction. You will have to decide which algebra concept that you are going to apply to the ad. You will receive a daily grade for working in class. That is 100 points a week. Each entry must include the following:

You are to have 5 entries. Each entry must include the following:

- You are to use 5 different ads from 5 different parts of the paper (i.e. business, sale ads, weather, advertisements . . .)
- You are to use 5 different mathematical concepts (you may use concepts that are not listed)
- Use correct computations and units-if needed
- Include an example or a description

**** Part III is worth 100 points ****

Approval Form: All topics must be approved by _____.
If not, there is a _____ **deduction** on Part I of the project.

Name _____ **Date** _____

Topic: _____

Short Description: _____

_____

_____

_____

_____

_____

Approved: _____ **Not Approved:** _____

Signature: _____

Approval Form: All topics must be approved by _____.
If not, there is a _____ **deduction** on Part I of the project.

Name _____ **Date** _____

Topic: _____

Short Description: _____

_____

_____

_____

_____

_____

Approved: _____ **Not Approved:** _____

Signature: _____

GRADING RUBRIC PART I

"EXAMINING THE HERITAGE OF GEOMETRY"

Your grade for this project will be judged on the following criteria:

Topic for Approved by Deadline . . . . (10 points) _____

Number of deductions for grammatical errors. . . . .(-2 points) _____

Major contributions to mathematics. . . . . (25 points) _____

Describe what you learned from the research . . . . (20 points) _____

Met ALL criteria outlined the guide . . . . (10 points) _____

Presentation:

Length was within time frame . . . . (5 points) _____

Creative and interesting. . . . . (20 points) _____

Props (i.e. speech, power point). . . . . (10 points) _____

GRADING RUBRIC PART II

"LIVING IN A 3-D WORLD"

Your grade for this project will be judged on the following criteria:

Photograph #1:

Entry is neat, organized and creative. . . . . (5 points) _____
Wrote the formula and used correctly. . . . . (5 points) _____
Correct units and computations . . . . (5 points) _____
Gave description or example . . . . (5 points) _____

Photograph #2:

Entry is neat, organized and creative. . . . . (5 points) _____
Wrote the formula and used correctly. . . . . (5 points) _____
Correct units and computations . . . . (5 points) _____

Gave description or example . . . . (5 points) _____

Photograph #3:

Entry is neat, organized and creative. . . . . (5 points) _____
Wrote the formula and used correctly. . . . . (5 points) _____
Correct units and computations . . . . (5 points) _____
Gave description or example . . . . (5 points) _____

Photograph #4:

Entry is neat, organized and creative. . . . . (5 points) _____
Wrote the formula and used correctly. . . . . (5 points) _____
Correct units and computations . . . . (5 points) _____
Gave description or example . . . . (5 points) _____

Photograph #5:

Entry is neat, organized and creative. . . . . (5 points) _____
Wrote the formula and used correctly. . . . . (5 points) _____
Correct units and computations . . . . (5 points) _____
Gave description or example . . . . (5 points) _____

GRADING RUBRIC PART III

"USING ALGEBRA IN EVERYDAY LIFE"

Your grade for this project will be judged on the following criteria:

Ad #1:

Entry is neat, organized and creative. . . . . (5 points) _____
Used the appropriate algebra topic. . . . . (5 points) _____
Used the correct computation. . . . . (5 points) _____
Gave description or example . . . . (5 points) _____

Ad #2:

Entry is neat, organized and creative. . . . . (5 points) _____
Used the appropriate algebra topic. . . . . (5 points) _____
Used the correct computation. . . . . (5 points) _____
Gave description or example . . . . (5 points) _____

Ad #3:

Entry is neat, organized and creative.................................... (5 points) _____
Used the appropriate algebra topic.................................... (5 points) _____
Used the correct computation... (5 points) _____
Gave description or example .... (5 points) _____

Ad #4:

Entry is neat, organized and creative.................................... (5 points) _____
Used the appropriate algebra topic.................................... (5 points) _____
Used the correct computation... (5 points) _____
Gave description or example .... (5 points) _____

Ad #5:

Entry is neat, organized and creative.................................... (5 points) _____
Used the appropriate algebra topic.................................... (5 points) _____
Used the correct computation... (5 points) _____
Gave description or example .... (5 points) _____

CHAPTER 7

BREAKING IT DOWN: FACTORING QUADRATIC EXPRESSIONS

When it says find the factors of 24, what does it mean for you to do? Factors are numbers or terms you multiply together to get the product. Some factors of 24 are 6 and 4, 2 and 12, 3 and 8, 1 and 24. Can you think of any other factors of 24?_____

Well, here's one for you: What are the factors of 100? _____
_____

Expressions can be factored too. Let's look at $4x^2$. 1x and 4x, 2x and 2x, -1x and -4x, -2x and -2x. Another way we can say it: 1, 2, 2, 4, x, and x. I think you get the point. So let's move on.

Let's look at one: $4x^2 + 20x - 12$.

As you notice, we have more than one term. How many terms does this polynomial have? _____. So it is called a _____.

Let's start by "breaking up" each term:

Take the $4x^2$: What are the factors of 4? _____.

What are the factors of x^2? _____

Take the 20x: What are the factors of 20? _____. What are the factors of x? _____.

Take the -12: What are the factors of -12? _____. (Hint: write a negative one in front of all the factors).

What do all the 3 terms have in common? _____. (circle it!)

The common factor goes in the front. Everything that is not circled goes in the parentheses:
_____ (_____ + _____ + _____)

Here's another one: $7p^2 + 21$.

List the factors of $7p^2$: _____. List the factors of 21: _____

33

Circle what they have in common. The common factor goes out front.

_____ (_____ + _____)

Here's another one for you: $4w^2 + 2w$

List the factors of $4w^2$: _____. List the factors of $2w$: _____

Circle what they have in common. The common factor goes out front.

_____ (_____ + _____)

Here are a few for you to do:

1. **$3a^2 + 9$**

   List the factors of $3a^2$: _____. List the factors of 9: _____. Circle what they have in common. The common factor goes out front. _____ (_____ + _____)

2. **$5t^2 + 7t$**

   List the factors of $5t^2$: _____. List the factors of $7t$: _____. Circle what they have in common. The common factor goes out front. _____ (_____ + _____)

3. **$14y^2 + 7y$**

   List the factors of $14y^2$: _____. List the factors of $7y$: _____. Circle what they have in common. The common factor goes out front. _____ (_____ + _____)

4. **$27p^2 - 9p$**

   List the factors of $27p^2$: _____. List the factors of $9p$: _____.

Now, let's take a look at the quadratic trinomial:

We know that a trinomial has "3 terms." Quadratic trinomials are in the form **$ax^2 + bx + c$**, where a, b, and c are numbers. To find this trinomial, we are looking for the factors of a times c and the sum of b.

Let's look at a few together:

1. $X^2 + 8x + 7$: First, tell me a = _____, b = _____, c = _____.

   We want the factors of 7 that add up to 8: _____.
   So we get $x^2 + x + 7x + 7$. Let's factor $x^2 + x$: _____.
   Factor $7x + 7$: _____.
   Put what they have in common in the first set of parentheses:
   (_____ + _____)
   Put the terms outside the parentheses in the other: (_____ + _____)
   Our answer is (_____ + _____)(_____ + _____)

2. $X^2 - 6x + 8$: First, tell me a = _____, b = _____, c = _____. We want the factors of 8 that add up to -6: _____.

   So we get $x^2 - 2x - 4x + 8$. Let's factor $x^2 - 2x$: _____.
   Factor $-4x + 8$: _____.
   Put what they have in common in the first set of parentheses:
   (_____ + _____)
   Put the terms outside the parentheses in the other: (_____ + _____)
   Our answer is (_____ + _____)(_____ + _____)

3. $X^2 - x - 12$: First, tell me a = _____, b = _____, c = _____.

   We want the factors of -12 that add up to -1: _____.
   So we get $x^2 + 3x - 4x + 12$. Let's factor $x^2 + 3x$: _____.
   Factor $-4x + 12$: _____.
   Put what they have in common in the first set of parentheses:
   (_____ + _____)
   Put the terms outside the parentheses in the other: (_____ + _____)
   Our answer is (_____ + _____)(_____ + _____)

4. $3X^2 - 16x + 5$: First, tell me a = _____, b = _____, c = _____. We want the factors of 15 that add up to -16: _____.

   So we get $3x^2 - x - 15x + 5$. Let's factor $3x^2 - x$: _____.
   Factor $-15x + 5$: _____.
   Put what they have in common in the first set of parentheses:
   (_____ + _____)
   Put the terms outside the parentheses in the other: (_____ + _____)
   Our answer is (_____ + _____)(_____ + _____)

CHECKING FOR UNDERSTANDING

You are going to be given some expressions to factor. Use the guidelines from the activity sheet to help you work out the problems.

1. $X^2 - 13x + 12$: First, tell me a = _____, b = _____, c = _____.

    a) We want the factors of 12 that add up to -13: _____.
    b) Rewrite the trinomial as 4 terms: _____.
    c) Let's factor the first two terms: _____
    d) Factor the second two terms: _____.
    e) Put what they have in common in the first set of parentheses:
    f) (_____ — _____)
    g) Put the terms outside the parentheses in the other: (_____ — _____)
    h) Our answer is (_____ — _____)(_____ — _____)

2. $X^2 - 7x + 12$: First, tell me a = _____, b = _____, c = _____.

    a) We want the factors of 12 that add up to -7: _____.
    b) Rewrite the trinomial as 4 terms: _____.
    c) Let's factor the first two terms: _____
    d) Factor the second two terms: _____.
    e) Put what they have in common in the first set of parentheses:
    f) (_____ — _____)
    g) Put the terms outside the parentheses in the other: (_____ — _____)
    h) Our answer is (_____ — _____)(_____ — _____)

3. $X^2 - 8x + 12$: First, tell me a = _____, b = _____, c = _____.

    a) We want the factors of 12 that add up to -8: _____.
    b) Rewrite the trinomial as 4 terms: _____.
    c) Let's factor the first two terms: _____
    d) Factor the second two terms: _____.
    e) Put what they have in common in the first set of parentheses:
    f) (_____ + _____)
    g) Put the terms outside the parentheses in the other: (_____ + _____)
    h) Our answer is (_____ + _____)(_____ + _____)

4. $X^2 + 16x + 28$: First, tell me a = _____, b = _____, c = _____.

    a) We want the factors of 28 that add up to 16: _____.
    b) Rewrite the trinomial as 4 terms: _____.

c) Let's factor the first two terms: _____

d) Factor the second two terms: _____.

e) Put what they have in common in the first set of parentheses:

f) (_____ + _____)

g) Put the terms outside the parentheses in the other: (_____ + _____)

h) Our answer is (_____ + _____)(_____ + _____)

5. $X^2 + 12x + 36$: First, tell me a = _____, b = _____, c = _____.

a) We want the factors of 36 that add up to 12: _____.

b) Rewrite the trinomial as 4 terms: _____.

c) Let's factor the first two terms: _____

d) Factor the second two terms: _____.

e) Put what they have in common in the first set of parentheses:

f) (_____ + _____)

g) Put the terms outside the parentheses in the other: (_____ + _____)

h) Our answer is (_____ + _____)(_____ + _____)

6. $X^2 - 4x + 3$: First, tell me a = _____, b = _____, c = _____.

a) We want the factors of 3 that add up to -4: _____.

b) Rewrite the trinomial as 4 terms: _____.

c) Let's factor the first two terms: _____

d) Factor the second two terms: _____.

e) Put what they have in common in the first set of parentheses:

f) (_____ + _____)

g) Put the terms outside the parentheses in the other: (_____ + _____)

h) Our answer is (_____ + _____)(_____ + _____)

7. $X^2 + 14x + 33$: First, tell me a = _____, b = _____, c = _____.

a) We want the factors of 33 that add up to 14: _____.

b) Rewrite the trinomial as 4 terms: _____.

c) Let's factor the first two terms: _____

d) Factor the second two terms: _____.

e) Put what they have in common in the first set of parentheses:

f) (_____ + _____)

g) Put the terms outside the parentheses in the other: (_____ + _____)

h) Our answer is (_____ + _____)(_____ + _____)

8. $3X^2 - 11x + 6$: First, tell me a = _____, b = _____, c = _____.

a) We want the factors of 18 that add up to -11: _____.

b) Rewrite the trinomial as 4 terms: _____.
c) Let's factor the first two terms: _____
d) Factor the second two terms: _____.
e) Put what they have in common in the first set of parentheses:
f) (_____ + _____)
g) Put the terms outside the parentheses in the other: (_____ + _____)
h) Our answer is (_____ + _____)(_____ + _____)

9. $X^2 + 19x + 48$: First, tell me a = _____, b = _____, c = _____.

a) We want the factors of 48 that add up to 19: _____.
b) Rewrite the trinomial as 4 terms: _____.
c) Let's factor the first two terms: _____
d) Factor the second two terms: _____.
e) Put what they have in common in the first set of parentheses:
f) (_____ + _____)
g) Put the terms outside the parentheses in the other: (_____ + _____)
h) Our answer is (_____ + _____)(_____ + _____)

10. $4X^2 - 8x + 4$: First, tell me a = _____, b = _____, c = _____.

a) We want the factors of 16 that add up to -8: _____.
b) Rewrite the trinomial as 4 terms: _____.
c) Let's factor the first two terms: _____
d) Factor the second two terms: _____.
e) Put what they have in common in the first set of parentheses:
f) (_____ + _____)
g) Put the terms outside the parentheses in the other: (_____ + _____)
h) Our answer is (_____ + _____)(_____ + _____)

THE FUNCTION THAT SMILES AND FROWNS AT YOU: THE PARABOLA

Most of you have kicked a football, played football, or watched football on television. I know you have never thought about the path of the football. Well, when kick the ball, it goes up and comes back down. What shape does the path of the football make?

Does it look something like this?

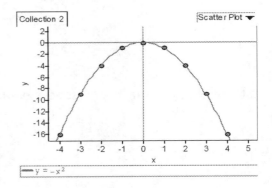

Have you ever watched a skateboarder? He starts at the top of the ramp and has to generate enough momentum to end up on the other side of the ramp. What shape does the path of the skateboarder create?

Does it look something like this?

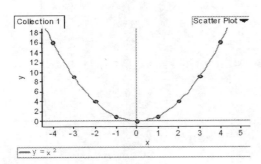

We can also think of a parabola like this. In the second example, the parabola looks like a smile. In the first example, the parabola looks like a frown. Can you tell me why example one is a "frown" and example two is a "smile"? (Hint: it has something to do with the sign in front of the function)

Ok, here's another way you can think at parabolas. One of the examples reaches a high point and then comes back down. It is similar to a mountain peak. The other example has a low point. It is similar to a valley. The vertex of a parabola is the highest point or lowest point of the parabola.

So let's look at some parabolas:

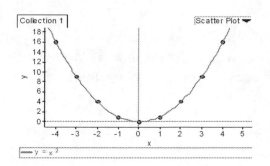

Here is a table of values that represent the parabola above.

	x	y	y2	<new>
1	-4	16		
2	-3	9		
3	-2	4		
4	-1	1		
5	0	0		
6	1	1		
7	2	4		
8	3	9		
9	4	16		

Collection 1

1. What is the domain of the function?

2. What is the range of the function?

3. What do you notice about the range values of the function $f(x) = x^2$?

4. Is the function look like a valley or a mountain peak?

5. So, is it the highest point or the lowest point? (*It is the y-value column*)

6. Find that ordered pair in the table and write it down. That point is the **vertex** of the parabola.

Let's look at another one:

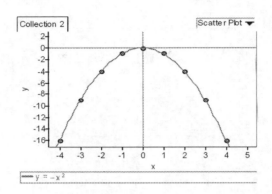

Now, let's look at a table of values for this parabola.

	x	y	y2	<new>
1	-4	16		
2	-3	9		
3	-2	4		
4	-1	1		
5	0	0		
6	1	1		
7	2	4		
8	3	9		
9	4	16		

Collection 1

1. What is the domain of this function?

2. What is the range of this function?

3. What do you notice about the range values of the function $f(x) = -x^2$?

4. Is the function look like a valley or a mountain peak?

5. So, is it the highest point or the lowest point? (It is the y-value column)

6. Find that ordered pair in the table and write it down. That point is the **vertex** of the parabola.

Not all parabolas are the same size. Some of them are "thinner" than others; some are "wider" than others.

Here's an example:

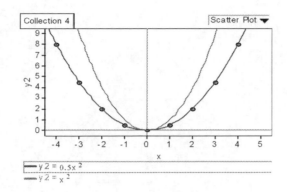

Here is a table of values for the function for the two graphs.

	x	y2	y	<new>
1	-4	32	16	
2	-3	18	9	
3	-2	8	4	
4	-1	2	1	
5	0	0	0	
6	1	2	1	
7	2	8	4	
8	3	18	9	
9	4	32	16	

Collection 3

What do you notice about the range values in y_2 and y?

Which graph grows faster, $y = x^2$ or $y = 2x^2$?

The graph that grows faster is "smaller." This is called a **vertical stretch**.

Let's take a look at this one:

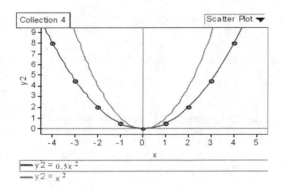

Here is a table of values for the two graphs.

	x	y2	y	‹new›
1	-4	32	16	
2	-3	18	9	
3	-2	8	4	
4	-1	2	1	
5	0	0 .	0	
6	1	2	1	
7	2	8	4	
8	3	18	9	
9	4	32	16	

Collection 3

What do you notice about the values in y and y_2?

Which graph grows "slower", $y = x^2$ or $y = 0.5x^2$?

The graph that grows "slower" is wider. This is called a **horizontal stretch**.

If the number in front of x^2 is greater than 1, what happens to the graph?

(*Hint: we are talking about these numbers . . . -4, -3, -2, . . . 2, 3, 4, . . .*)

If the number in front of x^2 is less than 1, what happens to the graph?

(*Hint: we are talking about positive and negative fractions*)

Now that you have completed today's activity, I have some questions I would like for you to answer.

1. Describe the shape of $f(x) = x^2$.

2. Describe the shape of $f(x) = -x^2$.

3. Tell me what the vertex of a parabola is.

4. Given the function $f(x) = 3x^2$, describe how it is related to $f(x) = x^2$.

Make a table for $f(x) = 3x^2$. How do the table values compare to those of $f(x) = x^2$?

Collection 5		
	x	y
1	-4	
2	-3	
3	-2	
4	-1	
5	0	
6	1	
7	2	
8	3	
9	4	

5. Given the function $f(x) = 0.25x^2$, describe how it is related to $f(x) = x^2$. Make a table for $f(x) = 0.25x^2$. How do the table values compare to those of $f(x) = x^2$?

Collection 5		
	x	y
1	-4	
2	-3	
3	-2	
4	-1	
5	0	
6	1	
7	2	
8	3	
9	4	

We have seen what happens when a number is written in front of $f(x) = x^2$. If the number is greater than 1, then we have a **vertical stretch** because the parabola is more narrow (it grows faster than $y = x^2$). If the number is less than 1—written as a fraction—we have a **horizontal stretch** because the parabola is wider (it grows slower than $y = x^2$).

Let's look at $f(x) = x^2$ again:

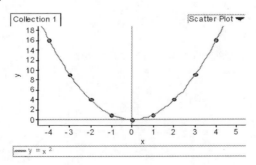

Now, look at this graph. Tell me what you notice about these two graphs.

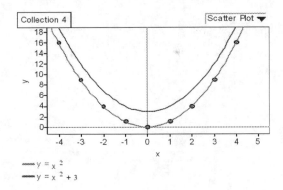

Fill in the table using your graphing calculator.

	x	y	<new>
1	-4		
2	-3		
3	-2		
4	-1		
5	0	3	
6	1		
7	2		
8	3		
9	4		

Collection 5

Tell me the vertex of $y = x^2$.

Now, for $y = x^2 + 3$, tell me the ordered pair that is the vertex of the parabola. This parabola has a new low point. This shift is called a vertical shift because the parabola can move up or down depending on the sign of the number after the x^2.

Let's look at $f(x) = x^2$ again:

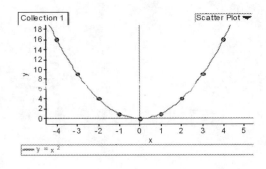

Let's look at this graph:

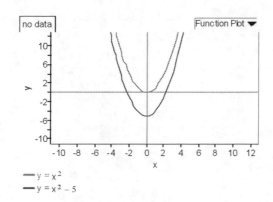

$y = x^2$
$y = x^2 - 5$

Tell me what you notice about these two graphs. Use your graphing calculator to graph the two parabolas above.

Use your graphing calculator to fill in the table.

Collection 6	x	y	y2	<new>
1	-4			
2	-3			
3	-2			
4	-1			
5	0	-5		
6	1			
7	2			
8	3			
9	4			

Tell me the vertex of $f(x) = x^2 - 5$.

Tell how the parabola shifted this time.

Ok, here's one more for you to look at:

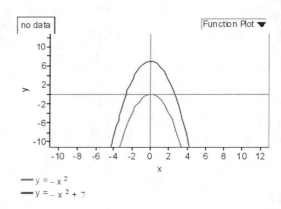

$y = -x^2$
$y = -x^2 + 7$

Using your graphing calculator to fill in the table for $y = -x^2 + 7$.

Collection 5	x	y
1	-4	
2	-3	
3	-2	
4	-1	
5	0	
6	1	
7	2	
8	3	
9	4	

Tell me the ordered pair that is the vertex of the parabola of $y = -x^2 + 7$.

Now, we just saw how a parabola can move up and down. Let's look at how a parabola left and right.

Let's look at the graph below:

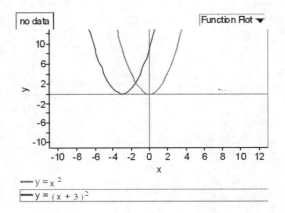

Tell me what you notice about the two parabolas in the graph. Use your graphing calculator.

Use your graphing calculator to fill in the table below.

Collection 1				
	x	y	y2	\<new\>
1	-4	16		
2	-3	9		
3	-2	4		
4	-1	1		
5	0	0		
6	1	1		
7	2	4		
8	3	9		
9	4	16		

Tell me what you notice at the vertices of the two parabolas.

This transformation is called a **horizontal shift** it moved to the left.

Now, let's look at another graph:

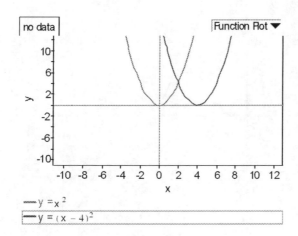

Tell me what you notice about these two parabolas.

Use your graphing calculator to fill in the table below:

Collection 1	x	y	y2	<new>
1	-4	16		
2	-3	9		
3	-2	4		
4	-1	1		
5	0	0		
6	1	1		
7	2	4		
8	3	9		
9	4	16		

Tell me about the vertices of these two parabolas.

Tell me why this parabola is called a **horizontal shift**.

Now, let's see if we can put it all together. Look at this formula: $f(x) = ax^2 + c$, where a and c are numbers.

1. Describe how you know when a parabola has a **vertical stretch**. Give two examples of parabolas that have a **vertical stretch**.

2. Describe how you know when a parabola has a **horizontal stretch**. Give two examples of parabolas that have a **horizontal stretch**.

3. What do you know if c is a positive number (i.e. $y = x^2 + 1$)?

4. What do you know if c is a negative number (i.e. $y = x^2 - 2$)?

CHECKING FOR UNDERSTANDING

Using your graphing calculator, type $y = x^2$ in y_1. Does x^2 have a low point or a high point?

_____

1. Name that ordered pair. _____

    In your graphing calculator, type $y = -x^2$ in y_1.

2. Does $-x^2$ have a low point or a high point? _____

3. Name that ordered pair. _____

4. The low point or high point of a parabola is called the _____.

    In your graphing calculator, type x^2 in y_1 and type $3x^2$ in y_2.

5. Is $2x^2$ smaller or wider than x^2? _____

6. This transformation is called a _____.

    In your graphing calculator, type x^2 in y_1 and type $5x^2$ in y_2.

7. Is $5x^2$ smaller or wider than x^2? _____

8. This transformation is called a _____.

    In your graphing calculator, type x^2 in y_1 and type $0.25x^2$ in y_2.

10. Is $0.25x^2$ smaller or wider than x^2? _____

11. This transformation is called a _____.

    In your graphing calculator, type x^2 in y_1 and $x^2 + 2$ in y_2.

12. In what direction does $x^2 + 2$ move? _____

13. How many units does $x^2 + 2$ move? _____

14. This transformation is called a _____.

    In your graphing calculator, type x^2 in y_1 and type $x^2 + 6$ in y_2.

15. In what direction does $x^2 + 6$ move? _____

16. How many units does $x^2 + 6$ move? _____

17. This transformation is called a _____.

   In your graphing calculator, type x^2 in y_1 and type $x^2 - 6$ in y_2.

18. In what direction does $x^2 - 6$ move? _____

19. How many units does $x^2 - 6$ move? _____

20. This transformation is called a _____.

In your graphing calculator, type $x^3 - 4x^2 + 2$ in y_1. Draw the function $f(x) = x^3 - 4x^2 + 2$ in the graph below:

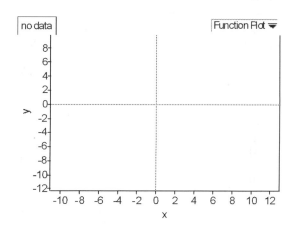

Describe the shape of this polynomial.

The last polynomial we will look today is $f(x) = 2x^4 - 3x^3 + x - 1$. This polynomial is **quartic**. What is the highest exponent of this polynomial? _____. This polynomial is **quartic** because it has an x^4 term.

In your graphing calculator, type $2x^4 - 3x^3 + x - 1$ in y_1. Draw the function $f(x) = 2x^4 - 3x^3 + x - 1$ in the graph below:

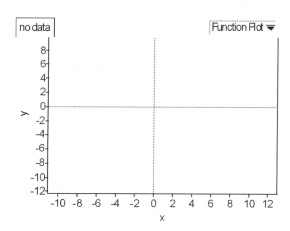

Describe the shape of the polynomial.

CHECK FOR UNDERSTANDING

Now we have looked at the many faces of the polynomial. Now it's your turn. For each graph I am going to give you one of the faces to draw.

1. You are to write an original polynomial. (You cannot use the examples I gave you in the activity)

2. In your graphing calculator, type your original polynomial in y_1.

3. Draw your original polynomial in the appropriate graph.

1. Cubic: f(x) = _____

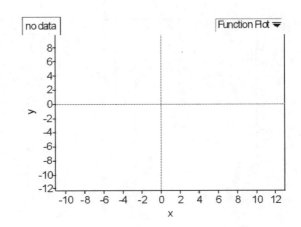

2. Constant f(x) = _____

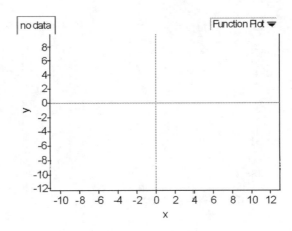

3. Quadratic: f(x) = _____

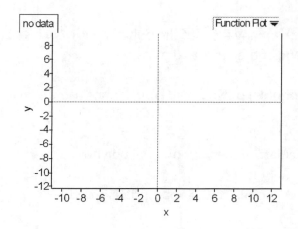

4. Quartic: f(x) = _____

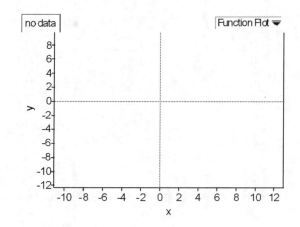

5. Linear: f(x) = _____

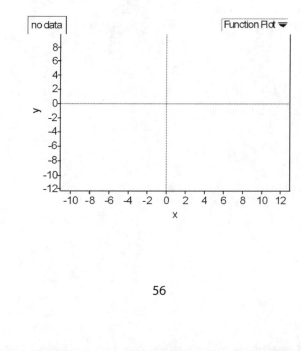

CHAPTER 9

SO WHO'S THE LEADER OF THE HOUSE?

Every polynomial has a leader. Let's look at $f(x) = 4x - 5$. What kind of polynomial is this function? _____. The **degree** of a polynomial is the highest exponent. What is the highest exponent of $f(x) = 4x - 5$? _____. So the **degree** of the polynomial is 1.

Polynomials should be written in descending order. The highest exponent should go first and count down from there.

Let's look at one: $3x^3 + x^2 - 4x + 2x^3$. What kind of polynomial is this function? _____.

Remember we talked about five kinds of polynomials in the first part of activity. I will give you a hint, one is constant.

Name the other four kinds of polynomials:

1) _____

2) _____

3) _____

4) _____

What is the highest exponent of $3x^3 + x^2 - 4x + 2x^3$? _____. There are two terms with the highest exponent! No problem, add them together: $3x^3 + 2x^3 =$ _____.

What is the degree of the polynomial? _____.

Put them in order from largest exponent to smallest exponent:

_____ + _____ + _____.

What is the number in front of the highest exponent? _____. This is called the **leading coefficient**. A **coefficient** is a number in front of a **variable**.

Here are a few for you to do:

1. $6 - 2x^5$.

  a) What is the highest exponent of this polynomial? _____.

57

    b) What is the degree of the polynomial? _____.

    c) Put them in order from largest exponent to smallest exponent: _____ + _____.

    d) What is the leading coefficient? _____.

2. $x^2 - 4x + 3x^3 + 2x$.

    a) What kind of polynomial is this function? _____.

    b) What is the highest exponent of this polynomial? _____.

    c) What is the degree of the polynomial? _____.

    d) Put them in order from largest exponent to smallest exponent: _____ + _____ + _____.

    e) What is the leading coefficient? _____.

3. $2m^2 - 3 + 7m$.

    a) What kind of polynomial is this function? _____.

    b) What is the highest exponent of this polynomial? _____.

    c) What is the degree of the polynomial? _____.

    d) Put them in order from largest exponent to smallest exponent: _____ + _____ + _____.

    e) What is the leading coefficient? _____.

4. $5a^2 + 3a^3 + 1$.

    a) What kind of polynomial is this function? _____.

    b) What is the highest exponent of this polynomial? _____.

    c) What is the degree of the polynomial? _____.

    d) Put them in order from largest exponent to smallest exponent: _____ + _____ + _____.

    e) What is the leading coefficient? _____.

5. $-x^3 + x^4 + x$.

    a) What kind of polynomial is this function? _____.

    b) What is the highest exponent of this polynomial? _____.

    c) What is the degree of the polynomial? _____.

    d) Put them in order from largest exponent to smallest exponent: _____ + _____ + _____.

    e) What is the leading coefficient? _____.

DEMONSTRATE YOUR UNDERSTANDING

Now we have talked about the parabola and the four transformations.

1. Name the four transformations:

    Using your graphing calculator, type x^2 in y_1 and type $-2(x + 5)^2$.

2. The -2 in the front causes the parabola to:
    a) turn into a frown
    b) turn into a frown and get smaller
    c) get smaller

3. The 5 in the parentheses causes the parabola to:
    a) move 5 places to the left
    b) move 5 places to the right
    c) move 5 places down
    d) move 5 places up

    Using your graphing calculator, type x^2 in y_1 and type $3(x - 4)^2 - 8$ in y_2.

4. The 3 in the front of the function causes the parabola to:
    a) get smaller by a factor of 3
    b) get wider by a factor of 3

5. The -4 in the parentheses causes the parabola to:
    a) move 4 places to the right
    b) move 4 places to the left
    c) move 4 places up
    d) move 4 places down

6. The -8 on the end of the parabola causes it to:
    a) move down 8 units
    b) move up 8 units
    c) move to the right 8 units
    d) move to the left 8 units

    Here's a function: $f(x) = 2x^2 - 4x^3 + x$

7. This function has how many terms? _____

8. What kind of "nomial" is this? _____

9. What kind of polynomial is this? _____

10. What is the highest exponent of this polynomial? _____

11. What is the degree of the polynomial? _____

12. Write the terms of the polynomial in order from the largest exponent and the smallest exponent.

    Here's a function: $f(x) = 2x^4 - 3x^2$

13. This function has how many terms? _____

14. What kind of "nomial" is this? _____

15. What kind of polynomial is this? _____

16. What is the highest exponent of this polynomial? _____

17. What is the degree of the polynomial? _____

18. Write the terms of the polynomial in order from the largest exponent and the smallest exponent.

    Here's a function: $f(x) = 6x$

19. This function has how many terms? _____

20. What kind of "nomial" is this? _____

21. What kind of polynomial is this? _____

22. What is the highest exponent of this polynomial? _____

23. What is the degree of the polynomial? _____

24. Write the terms of the polynomial in order from the largest exponent and the smallest exponent.

FINDING THE SOLUTIONS TO THE QUADRATIC EQUATIONS

We talked about solving factoring quadratic expressions. An **expression** does not have an equal sign. Today, however, we are going to be solving quadratic equations. So let's start with something simple:

1. $4x^2 = 256$.

    The first thing we want to do is eliminate the number in front of x^2. What do we need to do? _____.

    Now, we have $x^2 = 64$. To solve for x we need to take the square root $\sqrt{\ }$ of both sides.

    When you take $\sqrt{\ }$ of both sides what do you get? X = _____, x = _____. You get two solutions because $8^2 = 64$ and $(-8)^2 = 64$.

    Here are a few more for you to do:

2. $8x^2 = 512$. What do you do first? _____

    So now we have _____. Next, you take $\sqrt{\ }$ of both sides.

    Now we have x = _____, x = _____.

3. $4x^2 - 53 = 47$. This one is a little different. You must get rid of the -53 first. How do you do that? _____

    So now we have _____.

    Then you get rid of the 4 by _____. Now we have _____.

    Then you take $\sqrt{\ }$ of both sides. Now we have x = _____, x = _____.

4. $4x^2 - 28 = 8$. You must get rid of the -28 first. How do you do that? _____

    So now we have _____.

    Then you get rid of the 4 by _____. Now we have _____.

    Then you take $\sqrt{\ }$ of both sides. Now we have x = _____, x = _____.

Well, that wasn't too bad. However, there are some quadratic equations that require more work that those.

For these equations in the form $ax^2 + bx + c$, we can use the quadratic formula:

$$x = \frac{-b \pm \sqrt{b^2 - 4a}}{2a}$$, where a, b and c are **NUMBERS**!

Let's look at one:

1. $x^2 - 2x - 3 = 0$.

    Tell me a = _____, b = _____, c = _____.

    Now we want to substitute a, b and c into the formula: $\dfrac{-(2) \pm \sqrt{(-2)^2 - 4(1)(-3)}}{2(1)}$

    You can finish this one . . .

    We get two solutions: x = _____, x = _____.

2. $3x^2 - x - 4 = 0$.

    Tell me a = _____, b = _____, c = _____.

    Now we want to substitute a, b and c into the formula: $\dfrac{-(\ ) \pm \sqrt{(\ )^2 - 4(\ )(\ )}}{2(\ )}$

    And you can finish up the problem . . .

    We get two solutions: x = _____, x = _____.

3. $x^2 + 3x + 1 = 0$.

    Tell me a = _____, b = _____, c = _____.

    Now we want to substitute a, b and c into the formula: $\dfrac{-(\ ) \pm \sqrt{(\ )^2 - 4(\ )(\ )}}{2(\ )}$

    And you can finish up the problem . . .

    We get two solutions: x = _____, x = _____.

4. $x^2 + 2x - 1 = 0$.

Tell me a = _____, b = _____, c = _____.

Now we want to substitute a, b and c into the formula: $\dfrac{-(\ )\pm\sqrt{(\ )^2-4(\ )(\ )}}{2(\ )}$

And you can finish up the problem . . .

We get two solutions: x = _____, x = _____.

5. $3x^2 + x - 1 = 0$.

Tell me a = _____, b = _____, c = _____.

Now we want to substitute a, b and c into the formula: $\dfrac{-(\ )\pm\sqrt{(\ )^2-4(\ )(\ )}}{2(\ )}$

And you can finish up the problem . . .

We get two solutions: x = _____, x = _____.

6. $x^2 + x - 8 = 0$.

Tell me a = _____, b = _____, c = _____.

Now we want to substitute a, b and c into the formula: $\dfrac{-(\ )\pm\sqrt{(\ )^2-4(\ )(\ )}}{2(\ )}$

And you can finish up the problem . . .

We get two solutions: x = _____, x = _____.

7. $x^2 - 6x - 13 = 0$.

Tell me a = _____, b = _____, c = _____.

Now we want to substitute a, b and c into the formula: $\dfrac{-(\ )\pm\sqrt{(\ )^2-4(\ )(\ )}}{2(\ )}$

And you can finish up the problem . . .

We get two solutions: x = _____, x = _____.

ARE THESE YOUR FINAL ANSWERS?
FINDING SOLUTIONS TO QUADRATIC EQUATIONS BY GRAPHING

We have been looking at quadratic trinomials. We know the exponent on a **quadratic polynomial** is _____. This means it can up to 2 solutions. The most effective way for us to solve quadratic equations is to use the graphing calculator. The standard form of a quadratic equation is $ax^2 + bx + c = 0$.

When graphing quadratic equations in the graphing calculator, we want the equation to read "$ax^2 + bx = c$". In other words, we want the constant on the right side of the equal sign.

So let's look at one: $x^2 - 4x + 3 = 0$. We first have to subtract 3 from both sides of the equation. So now we have $x^2 - 4x = -3$.

In your graphing calculator, type $x^2 - 4x$ in y_1 and type -3 in y_2, Press GRAPH.

How many times does the line intersect the parabola? _____. So how many solutions do you have? _____.

To find the intersection points you press 2nd TRACE, Go down to #5 (INTERSECTION), press ENTER three times.

To get the second solution, you have to press TRACE to move the cursor. Hit the TRACE key until the cursor is on the other intersection point.

Now press 2nd TRACE, Go down to #5 (INTERSECTION), press ENTER three times. So $x =$ _____, $x =$ _____.

Now for each of the following quadratic equations, we want to find the solutions by using your graphing calculator. The steps are listed above.

1. $x^2 + 8x + 12 = 0$. What do you need to do first? _____.
    Now you are ready to type it in the graphing calculator.
    $x =$ _____, $x =$ _____.

2. $2x^2 + 5x - 7 = 0$. What do you need to do first? _____.
    Now you are ready to type it in the graphing calculator.
    $x =$ _____, $x =$ _____.

3. $3x^2 + 2x - 1 = 0$. What do you need to do first? _____.
    Now you are ready to type it in the graphing calculator.
    $x =$ _____, $x =$ _____.

4. $x^2 + 10x = 25$. What do you need to do first? _____.
   Now you are ready to type it in the graphing calculator.
   $x =$ _____, $x =$ _____.

5. $2x^2 + 3x - 5 = 0$. What do you need to do first? _____.
   Now you are ready to type it in the graphing calculator.
   $x =$ _____, $x =$ _____.

6. $x^2 = 3x - 1$. What do you need to do first? _____.
   Now you are ready to type it in the graphing calculator.
   $x =$ _____, $x =$ _____.

7. $8x^2 - 2x - 3 = 0$. What do you need to do first? _____.
   Now you are ready to type it in the graphing calculator.
   $x =$ _____, $x =$ _____.

8. $3x^2 - 4x - 2 = 0$. What do you need to do first? _____.
   Now you are ready to type it in the graphing calculator.
   $x =$ _____, $x =$ _____.

9. $x^2 + 6x - 5 = 0$. What do you need to do first? _____.
   Now you are ready to type it in the graphing calculator.
   $x =$ _____, $x =$ _____.

10. $9x^2 + 12x - 5 = 0$. What do you need to do first? _____.
    Now you are ready to type it in the graphing calculator.
    $x =$ _____, $x =$ _____.

Now, as we have stated previously that a quadratic equation can have UP TO 2 solutions. This also means a quadratic equation may have one solution or NO SOLUTION. The **discriminant** tells us the number of solutions a quadratic equation has.

The standard form of a quadratic equation is _____. We use **$b^2 - 4ac$** to find the **discriminant** of a quadratic equation.

We are some guidelines we need to follow for the **discriminant**:

- If $b^2 - 4ac > 0$ then the parabola has two real number solutions. That means the line intersects the parabola twice.
- If $b^2 - 4ac = 0$ then the parabola has one real number solutions. That means the line intersects the parabola once.

- If $b^2 - 4ac < 0$ then the parabola has no real solution; it has imaginary roots. That means the line does not intersect the parabola.

So let's look at one: $x^2 + 4x + 5 = 0$. There are two ways to find the **discriminant**. We can graph it in the calculator or you can use $b^2 - 4ac$.

1. Let's look at graphing: type _____ in y_1. type _____ in y_2.

   The line intersects the parabola how many times? _____. How many solutions does the parabola have? _____.

2. Let's look at $b^2 - 4ac$: a = _____, b = _____, c = _____.

   $(\ )^2 - 4\,(\ )(\ )$. _____.

   Is this number greater than zero, less than zero or equal to zero? _____.

   How many solutions does this parabola have? _____.

For each of the following, determine the number of solutions it has by using the **discriminant.** You can use either of the two methods used above.

1. $x^2 + 4x + 5 = 0$

2. $x^2 - 4x - 5 = 0$

3. $4x^2 + 20x + 25 = 0$

4. $2x^2 + x + 28 = 0$

CHECKING YOUR UNDERSTANDING

For each of the following quadratic equations, find their solutions by using the graphing calculator.

1. $2x^2 - 5x - 3 = 0$ x = _____ , x = _____ .

2. $3x^2 - 10x + 5 = 0$ x = _____ , x = _____ .

3. $6x^2 - 5x - 1 = 0$ x = _____ , x = _____ .

4. $7x^2 - x - 12 = 0$ x = _____ , x = _____ .

5. $5x^2 + 8x - 11 = 0$ x = _____ , x = _____ .

6. $4x^2 + 4x = 22$ x = _____ , x = _____ .

7. $2x^2 + x = \frac{1}{2}$ x = _____ , x = _____ .

For each of the following quadratic equations, determine the number of solutions by using the discriminant.

8. $2x^2 + 7x - 15 = 0$

9. $6x^2 - 2x + 5 = 0$

10. $2x^2 + 7x = -6$

11. $x^2 - 12x + 36 = 0$

THE COUPON AND THE DISCOUNT: COMPOSITION OF FUNCTIONS

Terrance works at Kroger. He gets a 10% employee discount. On his day off, Terrance goes grocery shopping. He buys two cans of Rotell for $0.99 each, a bag of Tortilla chips for $2.99, some ground beef for $3.99, and Velveeta for $4.97. He has a coupon for a $1.00 off the Velveeta.

1. Determine how much money Terrance is going to spend at Kroger. You must show ALL your work.

2. Show how much Terrance's grocery bill is when his 10% employee discount is applied AND then the $1.00 coupon is used.

3. Write a function that represents the employee discount.

4. Write a function that represents the $1.00 coupon.

5. Terrance decides to buy two 2 liters of Pepsi. Each liter is $1.69. Use the function in #3 to show much Terrance will spend for the two 2 liters of Pepsi.

You are looking through the sales paper. You see that Foot Locker is having a two-day shoe extravaganza. All shoes in the store are 25% the original retail price. You can save an extra $20 if you make a purchase of $100 or more. You decide to buy some shoes that cost $174.99.

1. Determine how much you will spend of YOUR shoes. You must SHOW all your work to receive credit.

2. Determine how much you will make if you buy some running shoes for $149.99.

3. Write a function that represents the 25% discount off the retail price.

4. Write a function that represents the $20 off a purchase of $100 or more.

5. Write a function that represents the 25% discount AND the $20 discount on select purchases.

6. You decide to buy a pair of shoes for you and your sister. Your shoes cost $149.99 and your sister's shoes cost $69.99. Use the function you wrote in #5 to show how much you will spend at Foot Locker.

APPENDIX

REFLECTION

1. What is the name of today's activity?

2. In about 3 or 4 lines, describe what the activity was about?

3. What math skills did you use today?

4. What did you learn today?

5. What was the goal of the activity? Did we achieve our goal today?

6. What did you like about the activity?

   What did you dislike?

   What, if anything do you think we should do differently?

RUBRIC FOR SMALL CLASS DISCUSSIONS

It is important for students to effectively communicate their thoughts and ideas with their peers. In a cooperative learning group, you have the opportunity to share your knowledge with your fellow peers. If someone in the group does not understand, be patient and SHARE your knowledge so they too feel confident about the task at hand. Your goal is work together to come with a solution to the problem at hand. One person should not do all the work. EACH person is responsible for his or her learning but you are working TOGETHER to solve the problem. So again, I have created some guidelines so EACH person can successfully solve the problem.

Score	Scalar	Possible Points	Description
4	5	20	Group provides the correct answer and explanation OR Group members actively aide peers to the correct answer Note: Ensure that EACH group member understands the solution to the problem
3	5	15	Group provides the correct answer and some explanation OR Group members aide peers to the correct answer OR SOME of the group understands the solution to the problem
2	5	10	Group provides the correct answer with no justification OR Group gives the answers to the other members OR ONLY the leader understands the solution to the problem
1	5	5	Group provides some answer and the group is not working together. Each person doing his or her own thing. NO cooperation.

RUBRIC FOR WHOLE CLASS DISCUSSIONS

It is important for students to be able to effectively communicate their mathematical thoughts and ideas in a positive and constructive manner. To increase mathematical communication in our classroom, I have devised this rubric for class participation grades. Remember: Do not be afraid to give an incorrect answer. This is a learning process. I want you to LEARN from your mistakes and learn WHY it is incorrect so next time you WILL give the correct answer.

Score	Scalar	Possible Points	Description
4	5	20	Provide the correct answer and explanation OR Explain or show your peers why an answer is incorrect and provide the correct answer Note: (you must respect your fellow classmates. Any derogatory statements will cause you to forfeit your score of a 4)
3	5	15	Provide an answer and explanation OR Guide a fellow classmate to the correct answer OR Provide the correct answer with some explanation OR Explain why the answer is incorrect and provide some the correct answer
2	5	10	Provide the correct answer with no explanation OR Recognize a solution is incorrect with no justification
1	5	5	Rely on other students to provide the correct answers OR Fail to participate or pay attention during the group discussions
0	5	0	Sleep in class OR Fail to take notes